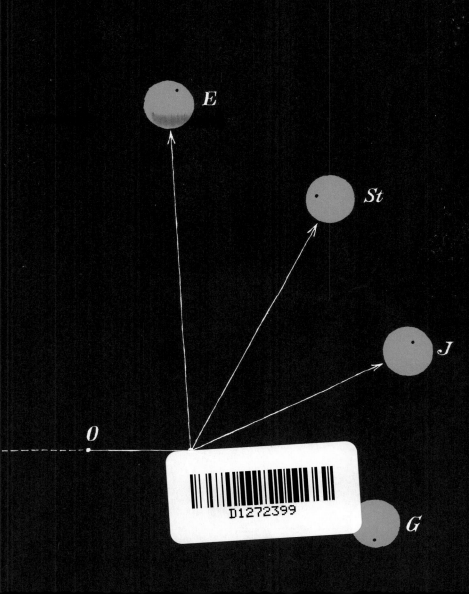

F   O

Peter F. Neumeyer & Edward Gorey
Why we have day and night

Pomegranate **kids**

For goodness sake!

It's all dark!

Ouch.

Oh.

What happened to the light?

Here, take my hand

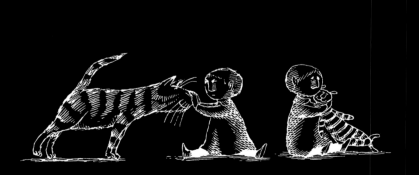

Could a squirrel have chewed a wire?

Did the ink spill?

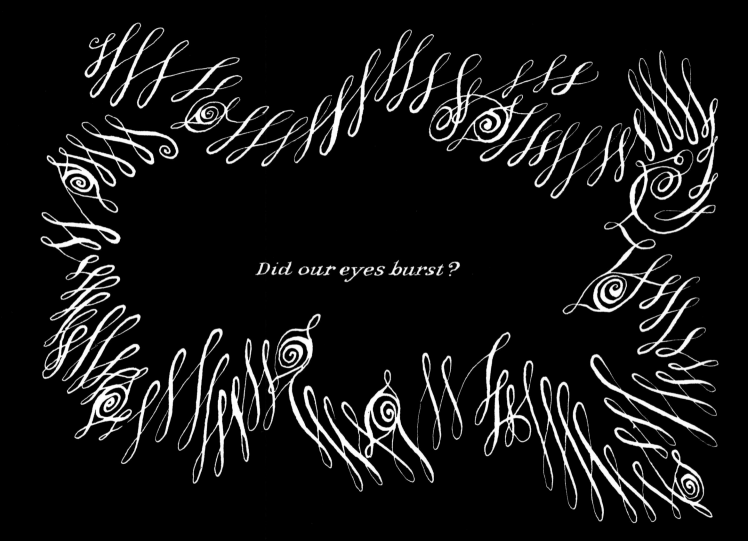

Did our eyes burst?

MATTHEW, MARK, LUKE, AND JOHN,
THE BED BE BLEST THAT I LIE ON.

Are we still asleep?

Are we in a cyclone?

Are we snails ?

Are we bats?

I know, we're underwater.

Aren't we born yet?

It's pitch black.

Do you know?

Why is everything black?

Certainly I know why everything is dark.
It is a long story.

Tell us!   *Tell us!*   *Tell us!*
Why is it dark?

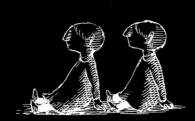

Remember when I asked Father
why the sun goes down. He said,
'It just looks like it goes down.

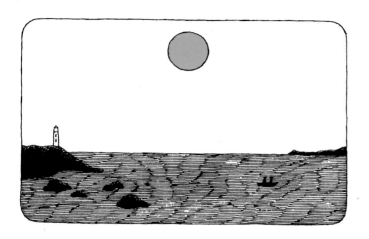

But really the sun does not go down.

'What really happens is that the earth turns around,' he said. He switched on a flashlight and I held an orange.

'Pretend you are a bug,' he said. 'And you are on the orange.

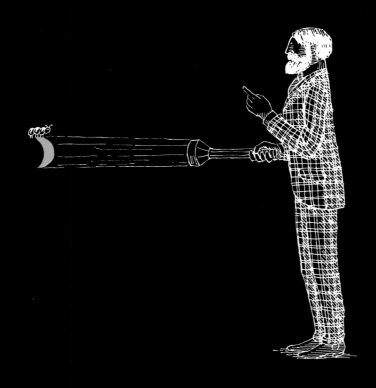

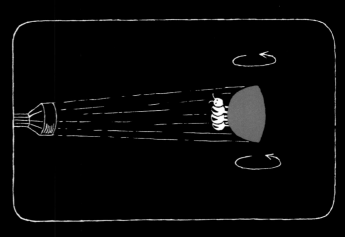

Now I spin the orange, just the way the earth spins. You see how the light shines on a different part of the earth all the time. First the bug is in the light — see!

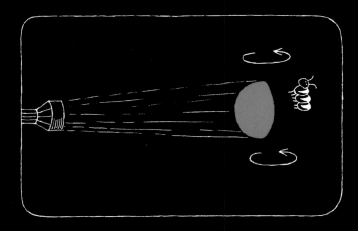

And now he is in the dark.'

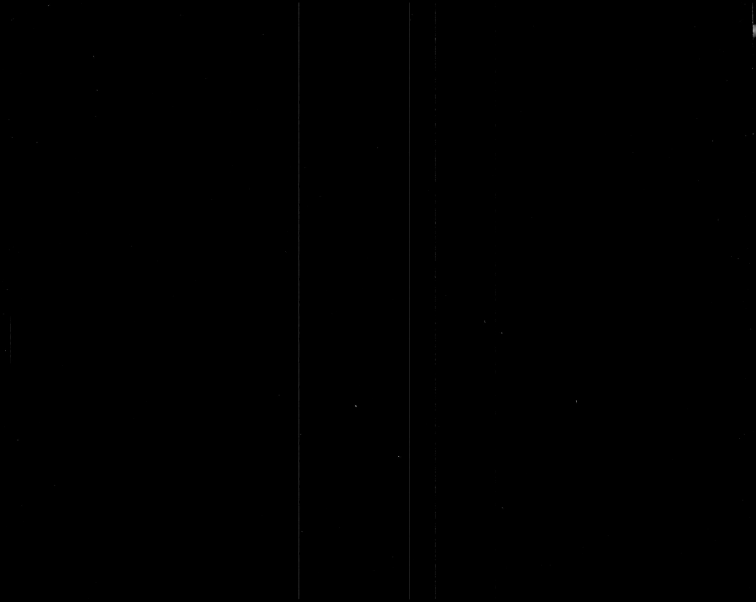

hy is it dark all over now?

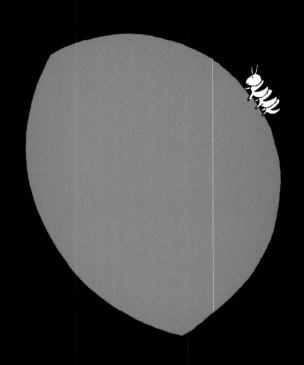

Because this little bug on the spinning
orange got hungrier and hungrier. The
hungrier he got, the more he would spin. And
the more he would spin, the hungrier he got.

And finally he got SO hungry that he ate
right through the outside, and into the
middle; and he crawled down deep inside
and it was all

all, all . . .

Published by Pomegranate Communications, Inc.
Box 808022, Petaluma CA 94975
800 227 1428 • www.pomegranate.com

Pomegranate Europe Ltd.
Unit 1, Heathcote Business Centre, Hurlbutt Road
Warwick, Warwickshire CV34 6TD, UK
[+44] 0 1926 430111 • sales@pomeurope.co.uk

This edition first published in 2011 by

Pomegranate **kids**®

This product is in compliance with the Consumer Product Safety Improvement Act of 2008 (CPSIA). A General Conformity Certificate concerning Pomegranate's compliance with the CPSIA is available on our website at www.pomegranate.com, or by request at 800 227 1428.

Library of Congress Control Number: 2010937850

ISBN 978-0-7649-5886-1

Pomegranate Catalog No. A196
Designed by Oky Sulistio

Printed in China

20 19 18 17 16 15 14 13 12 11   10 9 8 7 6 5 4 3 2 1

Other Edward Gorey books published by Pomegranate:

The Awdrey-Gore Legacy

The Black Doll: A Silent Screenplay by Edward Gorey

The Blue Aspic

Category

The Dong with a Luminous Nose, text by Edward Lear

The Eclectic Abecedarium

Edward Gorey: The New Poster Book

Elegant Enigmas: The Art of Edward Gorey,
    by Karen Wilkin

Elephant House: Or, the Home of Edward Gorey,
    by Kevin McDermott

The Evil Garden

The Gilded Bat

The Hapless Child

The Jumblies, text by Edward Lear

The Remembered Visit: A Story Taken from Life

The Sopping Thursday

The Twelve Terrors of Christmas, text by John Updike

The Utter Zoo: An Alphabet by Edward Gorey

The Wuggly Ump

Three Classic Children's Stories: Little Red Riding
    Hood, Jack the Giant-Killer, and Rumpelstiltskin,
    text by James Donnelly

and don't miss:

Edward Gorey's Dracula: A Toy Theatre

The Fantod Pack

The Wuggly Ump and Other Delights Coloring Book

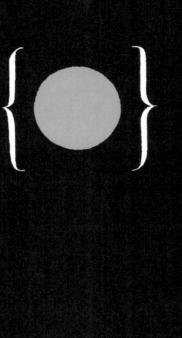

P